Close to the Tree

Poems by

Robert Gibbons

THREE ROOMS PRESS

NEW YORK CITY

Editor: Peter Carlaftes

Cover and Interior Design:
Kat Georges Design, New York, NY
katgeorges.com

Cover photos: Peter Carlaftes

First Edition

ISBN: 978-0-9884008-1-8

Printed in the United States of America.
Text set in Adobe Caslon.

Published by
Three Rooms Press, New York, NY
threeroomspress.com

CONTENTS

I dedicate this book to all the ancestors
that crossed the river:

Versie Lee Edwards
Minnie Lee Hansford
Delia Wilson
Liza Sherman
Mattie Gibbons
Evelyn Jackson
Lucy Hansford
Rosa Edwards

Close to the Tree

Home

who said we did not receive the death penalty at birth
our skins bruised by the Florida sun it is a race and
a bean field a trace and a sugar mill and yet
we are under control and submission the deadbeat
and the dark feet ones that dangle with arms of machetes
and you still do not understand there was no Glades Day
for us only night in purple stalks pink ghetto and blue stores
there are urinals on the outside tribunals for the smallest crimes
and there was no equality on the other side of lake shore I am not
sure I know fifty died with arthritis and fifty more on the dialysis
machine but all excuses are nailed to the cross the preacher says
well I do not believe everything the preacher says I had to
learn on my own and this is not easy I know segregation

I know reparation and you can never pay the migrants
enough the ones that drank water from the back of a corn
machine the ones that wrapped pork chop sandwiches in tin foil

and yes we toil for our children's children but this is not
the answer and you take it all away and you move far away
so you can't remember but look at the yearbook of the muck
hear the sound of cane truck at seven fifteen and you will see
my dream.

Florida

all these years we have this love-hate relationship;
as a child I played hide and seek among your cherries;
squirting red pepper into my eyes;
eating of your divine sunshine; now my mouth salivates as I
bite your naval ; suck every juice from your
citrus; I still nibble your breast, as rotund; as
profound as grapefruit; I claim you grand matriarch;
your silver locks reminds me of moss near the border;
as I ride your Biscayne back road in search of myself;
the promise to leave, but your roots are too deep;
the longing for you too steep

now my eyes water for Jacksonville's spine;
each curve as old as the Spanish ancestors;
as primitive as the doubloon; the little red school-
house that gave me berth; baptized me the fountain
of youth; kissing Tampa Bay's mouth; intersecting
the skyway

you, the southern woman; the eight hour ride down
your orgasm; from Tallahassee to Miami; from deciduous
to tropical; from heat to hotter; want to take my clothes
off on these topless Gould nights; the sand in the bottom
of my beach bag reminds me of you; still have your keys
to remind me the door awaits

tamarind

is the color
of my mother's womb
an oblong peninsula
jutting into the
Caribbean Sea
it colors the mangoes
as far as
Lake Okeechobee

call me Aunt Lily
of the valley
call me flood
the cemetery
call me cumquat
call me cherry
and lavender
call me aquamarine
call me out at
night before
the fireflies
light

it is the color
of her birth canal
it's swampy
it's saw grasses
it's honey
it's molasses
call me
Uncle Sammie
call me
Tamiami Trail

call me Apalachee
and manatee
strawberry
call me Wacissa
the pollen
honey bee

Elizabeth Bishop
Wallace Stevens
call her home

tell
Zora Neale
Hurston
she is stillborn
jump for her sun

call me back
to color
so
temperate
so simple
call me
everglade
call me to
the water
where turtle
eggs lie

call me
Sanibel
call me
Naples

call me
the city
of orchids
the bridge
to Singer Island
call me back
to church
call me palm
call me a
beach bag
call me
to her port

call me
Pahokee
call me
Loxahatchee
the Belle of
the Glades

hook

my grandmother would take us across
the Georgia line every summer
as if we were migrant workers
traveling the backroads
from Okeechobee to Tallahassee
chicken coops and fruit stands
elements change
from tropical to deciduous
dirt to clay
corn tobacco cotton
winding the black bottom

she would batter
dressing them in flour
smothering them in her power
placing them in rectangular pans
covered in aluminum foil
the toil of the gravy
packing us in her beige Buick
the Florida sun through it

she knew
she did not tell
she clears her mind of doubt
praying over the steering wheel
shifting to the right
making it there
before dark

Spirit

this morning I prayed for a poem
something similar to the gardener
hardly digging fresh earth to plant
the front sun hiding another day behind
curtains of clouds the listless wind
the crowd of song in my head there
still no word from yesterday as
I pillage the sidewalk for metaphor
am protective of this mission only
listen to the journey want the menagerie
of color the rudder of rustling water
the father of trickle and sprinkle of green
walking nowhere in between heaven
and earth blunder and mirth and in the
end the man said I did not see you
you are like spirit

like an angel he said the danger
of wanting more in these days
without words without girth it is trying
to see if it will come or the birds just
eating the salads of orange the burnt
noise of boredom is it a waste to
hasten this rush if so then make me
calm give me the balm I once had

as a child the mild-summer the barefoot
tumbler of white it's still a fight
a feat the beat of chirp the berth
to come back once again invention
the attention to this voice not to
overburden the sound but to
crown it in rhyme not the stymied
or the stigmata not the time
or the errata but this is spirit
the pirouette of etymology undulate
me waiting for the answer but
it was here before the prayer
it was just submission but the obligation
was to sit here and do it

barber

can only think of shaving cream between
me and the separation point between skin
and stubble between sky and land between
rock and river the thrills of clippers and dippers
flying apparitions all partition-superstition
grandmother said cover that mirror when it's
lightning come inside when the mosquitoes
are biting but it's unlimited and infamous sitting
in a barber's chair from way up there

the liberation of the peon
(for Diego Rivera)

it has been eighty years since the arrival
of Diego the crowd is immense the politics
still intense I smell the burning of the sienna
like the sugarcane in winter it is brown
on canvas we were all frozen assets
there are fresco covers in tarp—conceals
chips away can feel the revolution
sounds of a pneumatic drill growls
paints the rhythms of the American worker
the agrarian voice of Zapata forms
behind the mural panels then the depression
pencils in his sketchbook peasant laborers
with babies on their hips it is the peon
and the peonage the scion color mirages
my vantage points the flame inflames
the blame blasphemy look around for the dead
see Frida in her poster bed

Andrada
(for José Bonifácio de Andrada e Silva)

I know you miss me
but I was lost in the sound
it could be the cry
of the saxophone or the growl
of trombone Mingus
I am moanin'
I feel the Blue Monk
I went on a bop road-
trip to Alabama with Coltrane

I tried to understand the reason
I am communing with you
it's rather risky
to compromise the trope
on a common New York statue

if I had my choice it would be Mnemosyne
the goddess of memory
or Lincoln with his cloak and cape
like picking the garbage to cope
from a can at Union Square

I am where I am
and who is José Silva
to bring such a gift
if he is patriarch of Independence
for Brazil then raise Zumbi

I sit hear in silence
only the rhythms of the street sweeper
only Whitman's astronomer
in this backdrop of a busy Bryant park
maybe Andrada gave me a poem
in my pocket

Andrada in quiet reflection
in juxtaposition to Lincoln
his straightened coiffure and tuxedo
does not bother me
Andrada this Ellis Island harbor
receives you maybe he knows
more that you give him credit
instead we pass by like an Oppen sky-
scraper where we just look down

Andrada
in repetition his inhibitions
are mine as his singularity
he is isolated he is ostracized
with polished patina
his non-compromising demeanor
just keep moving
just keep standing

there is no blending among
the hedges
it's tough on a stone bench
looking for a lonely fix
and there are only fifteen minutes
Andrada gave me just
his is what I need

taking the long train home
(for James Arthur Baldwin)

sorry
James Baldwin
could not afford
the rare book
on Madison Avenue
could not afford
Blues for Mr. Charlie
could not sell
my soul to be published
could not
only going home
on the long train
but the words
of Winston Churchill
at the Morgan
and the buildings
in front are forging

could not
afford their price
can never
be concise
but can pay the cost
could not but
only walk
so they call

it a rare book
in the window
wrapped
in plastic
could not
afford
the preservation
paper could
assume
the weather
if this means
anything but

sorry James
taking the long
train home
taking all
the croons
and moans

taking
the long train
home
making it all
a song

drown in the city

one night
I slept on the streets
of Times Square
the rain fell
and I was in search of Junot
Diaz
drowning by the lights
the hotel with bed bugs
the cracks in the walls
the rain fell
just the covering
of my jacket
the sidewalk a mattress
just sitting there
as the audience left
the only feature
was me

Mean Streets
(for Piri Thomas)

people are coming out of Port Authority
like water, see them in a place;
that will spit them out like a cough;
they come because they are attracted to
the lights; they are attracted to Frank O'Hara's
idea of a walk; they are attracted to BBQs
and ten dollar shoes; just to say they bought
them; they are attracted to the idea of a marquee;
the little lightbulbs; encircling the sign;
they find themselves stranded on the corner;
with a suitcase and cell phone; they find
themselves with a pretzel and a hotdog;
with a newspaper and disappointment;
they find themselves stranded like
a shish kabob in a bun; in the middle
of this endless parade; upon hopes
that don't float; an illusion as back-door theater;

they will never be invited; they catch
a train bound for Brooklyn; through these
few streets that once held their dreams;
not long ago they could not afford
the subway peanuts; a few streets

of African men carrying signs of tour buses;
carrying pines for designer bags, but even
they can't understand; they only under-
stand one thing; it is as urgent as their
red vest; they will never be accepted;
they will never be asked to diversify;
they may be a target; because of their
table full of off brand; they too
are rebels against the system; a system
that will never respect them; for now
they are traffic tickets; a summons
a violation; through these few streets
that hold their dreams; they are another
collection and they will run
you over if you get in their way; these
few streets will take your picture; plaster
it all over the blotter; so you might as well
hold yourself down; in hell's kitchen;

walk away from fifteen minutes;
it's a waste of time; you can't afford me;
anyway. I am expensive; if I were you
I would find a diner; with a special;
because those fifteen minutes
repping will not save you

troutdale, oregon

it was as if I rode through a movie set
small framed transports of the west
they call them antiques and oddities
I call it death and obliquity
want to remember my old cap gun
and play cowboys and natives
can only see the haze
reminding me of an open fire
waiting for it to dissolve
where are the pounding of the fish
by the Wishram man
I want to be as happy as a papoose
it's only the beginning now
only the evergreens are gods
omniscient protrusions
hiking out the side of the mountains
lifting the burden of man-made
the Multnomah Falls
clocks us in her hourglass
they claim to hold on to the past
the last of the beaver pelts

there are natives for sale
but there are no natives
like the extinction of the salmon

the kind with instinct
going back to where they were born
the spawning the fighting upstream
why do we need a spillway
pulling twelve million gallons
per second I am bound in this gateway
to see the fish at the Bonneville Dam

Clinton Street

it was the clopping of Pradas
and Jimmy Choo-choo trains
I like being linear
other things will not intrude upon this work
but it was after the Delancey
the romance of dusty red curtains and no windows
hanging the floor the smell of gin and pineapple
the babble of women at Sarah Lawrence
it made me want a pizza
but this person with a Caesar
stripping my clothes seducing the verbs
the adjectives are irrelevant
I want to write about sex
and I like being linear
how certain people bed me in public
they can have all my hanging particles
but it was just another night in the village
the streets a cold sweat

the mini and the down low prowling the text
feeling too old just wanting to read a book
instead ran the streets with those much prettier
much younger those with V-necked little vests

wearing baseball caps and sunglasses
this poem is all about ass
I thought sucking a nipple
but there are no appearances
should I finally become religious

kingdom of land, sea, and sky

only one picture reminds me
of what I just left
for a few days now
the time changes to order
back to the East
the show business
of empire

to return to the didactic
the refractive light
the sun can't break through
on Times Square
the buildings leave us scraped
as they tower the air
as they occupy wall street
owning us with their dominance
and their prominence
possessing a few to
consume some their dreams

I though imagine the landscape
of New Amsterdam before the arrival
of the Dutch and all others who claim

sovereignty and seniority
the time of the beavers of the turtle
island blocks Clinton Castles
maps were not drawn by cartographers
and it was the native instinct
of Iroquois Nations
the Shinnecock
before Washington made his great
sojourn up the Delaware

had a chance to witness
the Hood and the Helen
of the West
and dis-coverable
place even this present time
to witness the sandstorms
of the forest off Pacific City
and enormous width
and breadth of the barks
of Grecian and the Douglas fir

no wonder Thomas Jefferson
sequestered Lewis and Clark
and their famous assistant York
to travel by keel boat

up the Mississippi
lands of accomplished beauty
the kind with fortitude
when breathing in the clouds at noon
rising to the sound of osprey
or the long-billed murrulet
and the American coot
it makes us feel differently
about the way we think and live
the way we take for granted the natural
more than us they are more beautiful
and more ancient
imagine counting the rings
in the bottom of a redwood
much of the forest had
been cut back
it had been commercialized

but there is still enough
Vista Point looking down
so far and it is all river
and mountain and cloud
until the dissolving of the haze
all I could do was journal

like Lewis and Clark
like Catlin like O'Keeffe
like Robert Colescott

had never seen the big feet
of Lincoln as big
as an Oregon oak
the breathtaking beauty
allays the fast pace
and in the words of Mark Twain
"I am the American"
whether marginalized
or scrutinized if I live on the
Delta or under the subway

I claim this land as Richard Wright
made the assertion before me
those of us who are interested
in persimmon trees or honeydew
or lemon yellow or the elk or
a rose garden
you must go and must seek and
taste you must find the grace

in your own reality for it is
big enough for all
that which stands like jagged rock
off Cape Meares the mysterious ledges
and lighthouse arouses us
it is from all our spheres
of influences and all other
aviaries and archipelagos
and cypress swamps and finally
it was the soil the muck that claims me
and it shall be forever more

a man with a black eye patch

stands every day
at the upper room
of the subway and me
with my Cave Canem tee
the subterfuge
in language
skirting the evidence
is no different than he
with his incessant gleaming
like reams of waste paper
filling the receptacle

the man
the black eye patch
the lashing of
his paper cup and his coins
his dribble and his song
his message for the economy
has no use for autonomy

if he only knew the respect
how he puts me into a
double check it is the beating
of the pavement

he is on his day job
as I rob him for metaphor
cop him for rhyme
each and every time

see him sleeping
in the park
see me reaping
in the dark
but this is not
an observation
it is a purification
about a recluse
being ostracized
the minutiae
and the sanctified

the patch keeps the
enemies out
it's a latch to
to stop sinning now
the man
with a black eye patch

can not be more proud
more confident
while I
a stunt
and rudiment
it's me and not he
with a deficiency
with all this pride
has no remedy

and no I am not
a victim but he's
a product of
the system

the man in
the black
eye patch
is the first
and I
a mask

monk's vintage thrift shop

I looked into the window of the vintage
all the rentals and storefronts are closed
going out of business to witness
such gentrification such bifurcation
but you're holding on like a gospel plow
tilling its fingers through the good book
the old-fashioned the antique the odd
the bizarre they say it will not be
another four years these people don't
care because they've never voted
never had hope in the government
in this boomtown gone bust in this
distrust of the white man all those people
on this dead end street the nouveau riche
with steel and glass with papier-mâché
and demitasse but what about the elderly
the geriatric the elasticity of holding

the shop moans like some Baptist hymnal
caught up in the raptures but it was me
mesmerized by the window full of cameras
full of bric-a-brac names with metric type
writers in orange Indian and voodoo dolls

it's the bowling shoes and tools unmanageable
did not have to be uptown to hear Harlem
calling but it was a fire in the ghetto the stilettos
are no longer sling backs it was my chance to fall
into a trance it was the pillaging of the east village
the war walking through and burning everything
in sight but I kept standing there as the crowd
congregates we all wanted to relate that this
is one of the last a past footnote all had been
done has been overrun so I tried to entertain
myself but the window just detained me

a woman with water

whatever happened
to the woman
in Union Square
the one
who sells water
her sounds barter
in voluminous liters

maybe she's
with Ahab
hunting Moby
maybe she's
transcended
like Rumi or
the Sufi
maybe she swims
to Atlantis

or to Muir
sailing with
Wallace Stevens
lost in the blur

she tables
her elements
H too O
exile
on an island
in the stranded
archipelago

it would not happen that this would be the month
it would not be the graduations and the dedications
it would not be the civil war and the memorial and we
preempt this for the election of a new president
for a new resident in the building but the change
came early and the rain stayed only a few days
and left forgotten like the umbrella instead the heat
her humidity the perfidy of time and I ran home
to hide myself the other self the one not on the day job
the one that comes after five o'clock during happy-
hour that stalls at the traffic light and closes the door
and wipes its hand after the unkempt and gauche
using sanitizer for everything thinking it will cure
ensure longevity but it will become another weak
end of shorts and trying to do all we can clumped into
all the groceries all the toiletries and the foibles
but hear it comes again and there it is on the morning
not sure if it is new because this never stops it's as long
as the last time I witnessed and pitched but it was the same
ennui

"I sinned against my talent"
(taken from Tony Bennett)

I am as blank
as tissue paper. The cracks in the floors
are my wounds. As if my great-
grandmother's bones are exhumed
The stairs are reliquary,
they creak, not certified.

then I come back; the construction
paper as deep as the diagram.
The laying of words
is like the laying on of hands. Its
chrism, its vision. They come clunky;
subjects without predicates;
their verbs do not agree; they are
book dependent; bound by text;
a lost lexicon.

it's the conquistadors in Mexico;
drowning in Junot; planting crosses
in Montezuma; its vocabulary

like bodega and comida; pushing
the Americas uptown; the diaspora
is brown, but the stone is blue.

I am crying. I hear the sounds
radiators from the upper levels
it cries. it wails as if the building
has birth pains. Her name is Julia
or Margaret. I am enforced. Enslaved
to a paycheck. Living within a mortgage.
a token by choice. see me. I am invisible.
I am a calendar with no dates. There
is no tissue paper, so I wipe it away
by hand. I am recycled. rehearsed.
disjointed creating sodden art into data.
It's all errata. It is all errata.

octopus tree

it was not the pin pricks of the pine needles
that captured my soul but it was the sitka spruce
it was the picea sitchensis that gives me anesthesia
it was the circumference of the trunk its limbs
and the height it was the timber and the light
it was the Natives that prayed there it was
the designated and the estimated it was the dream
I had of its tentacles that uplifted me into the spires
it became a keel of a slave ship carrying York
it became the perch and the peak the reach
and the doublespeak it was the debate and the debacle
the irate and the maniacal it was a hatchery and
the last remaining when I saw no central trunk
tried to debunk the log rollers the one bowling me
over holding to its heritage as it bled from stigmata
the mist will burn it was a holy sepulcher with
spiritualists from Utah they all had walking sticks
with all this congestion it was the octopus
the holiness amongst us

a temple of the holy ghost
(Babba Robert Gibbons-the-first)

again I ask where does voice
calm when does it supersede
flesh and bone I ask for an answer
for knowledge before the middle
passage as I sit before the door
of no return the estrangement
the arrangement of living word
of mouth but she was southern
southern and you were northern
was it played out in the family
legend when she begs you
to stay for the children
couldn't die with the first frost
of a Florida winter but it had
to be summer or was it the
arthritis that crept through
like a dirt road of Georgia
I inherited the marks on my face
on my shoulder from beyond
the name beyond the fame

where is this voice her singing voice
her love of literature the bitter septum
as old as Mason-Dixon wants to listen
to the other side of the story
wants to believe that you named me
for a reason your blood in this season
takes me back into your fatherly arms
calms this hurt on my tongue

a fruit stand somewhere on the east side

I know this is the city, but it was the moment
of passing the fruit stand I smelled you
with that combination of heat and lust, the
must of me peeling your sleeves down, licking
your clavicle your nape, I want to take and deflower
by undressing you , to expose then, I want to tease
the inside of the hull, I want to feel the push and
pull of hard labor, I feel like a sledge hammer
with the pressure of concrete on a construction
site, I want to bite each part of the flesh, until
the juice drips from the corner of my mouth,
that smell arouses me, the flavor of papaya
and a big bay leaf, did I not say to the core, I want
to bore a hole through it, I want to chew the cud
I want to stew in it like potpourri, then, I will take
the fat seed between teeth and yes I will be
your sloppy mess, it's hard to be a dangling
participle to a mango

point to point navigation
(for Gore Vidal)

there is it, that famous birthdate suddenly last summer, had the rare
opportunity to see you in the Barnes and Nobles on Union Square
being wheel-chaired across the room like some king; being ushered
to the front to sit audience but it is more than sharing the same
birthdate, it's about the words you left; the ambition, your face bell-
wethered; your lips discreet; your eyes the seat of power

some of us only read the history books, but suddenly; I hear
    the williwaw;
keeping company with Capote and Buckley; Mailer and
    James Baldwin;
we shy away from namedropping and famous friends but who's to know
if you decided not to reveal just revile; I imagine a conspiracy theory
words being pushed across the table like flan; the erudite eager for
    a duel
with Aaron Burr

my claim is my claim, but the claim is fame; there is a certain amount
of gentility, but who's to say gentility is all that; being well read is not
being well bred, St. Albans and Exeter are mere stanchions; are mere
placemats for literati but this body of work has glitterati; it reeks
    of gossip
and critical review; it peeks in hills of Hollywood and the
    urban scrawl
of Virginia

the revelation furtive, the subterfuge, the subtext; why not
a thespian flying through the canon with Lindbergh; why not a queer
muse-dom; an Elizabethan-Shakespearean swapping sonnets
with Christopher Isherwood and Tennessee Williams; lying
in bed with the same sex sex; not giving ourselves over
to monogamy, but the androgyny of time; not allowing the words
that describe us; the acerbic and prolific and polemic
is never enough, it's all political and why not it's all heretical
better to walk away; go on sabbatical; live in the cliff notes of margins;
the barter with destiny

"I am just as just as I appear," you once said; being blacklisted instead
but the craft is carcinogenic ; it just morphs into another form another
genre another agenda; and then we await for the valediction
    or benediction;
neither one may relate, neither one maybe our fate, but immortality,
    my son,
immortality

on a painted boat in misty rain
(for Su Dongpo)

listen
to the long poem
of the crabapple
while residing
on the painted boat
in misty rain
eye
sea smoke
devouring things
man-made
trees are
casting shade
upon my back
remaining grounded
to the East
but I am West now
of the Rockies
so concrete
I've left behind

as the boat sings
to me
the tranquility
of Luo Ping

the ability
of Xiaobo
red white
and blue
in mosaic
flowers
prosaic
with trickles
of sun

only four
characters reveal
ten-thousand
ravines
engulfed in
misty mountains

Riverside Drive

the fireflies drop
like asteroids
maybe they are immortal
a syzygy of
Ossie Davis
and Gil Scott-Heron
the Rose of Sharon
but the park along
the drive speaks
maybe Robert Hass
will name them
floribunda
or flummery
but I came
to a party
not for hisses
by a pale woman
at moonlight
there I was
with grass
as a mattress

had to use
my Adam's apple
to unravel
my lycanthropy

a remembrance
(for Valerie Conti)

when I walk into rehab
on the corner of Dean and Hoyt
the room opened its arms to me
as Mary stands there
the clerk became a deacon
ushering me upstairs
to the second floor
it became an upper room
I saw old people
people that told stories
with worry lines
and a hundred chances
to be disabled
people who have seen
some of the great wars
the depression the regret
of their generation
people who were geriatric
unprotected probably receiving
their social and their security

with a once a month checks
people with craters in their faces
once with the glory of the maker
but the hater of a carpal
a syndrome the criminality
of the elderly people
who gave candy to their
grandchildren may have been
members of a jury people
once sugar daddies that lost
their cane and now the latter
rain is all that's left
as I left the room
the weeping and the noisy
the cold and cozy
wheelchairs around the
space the place became
a purgatory of thought
the graying moss of their
hair pulled back behind scars
as I lowered myself
to the street
there is no relief insight
only the plight of living

hoping when the time
comes for me to enter
the upper room
someone like you
will be there

Grandpa with no name
(for Sammie Lee Edwards of South Bay, Florida)

for years we did not need to know it
he came home at five and his dinner
was hot like the Florida sun his legs
the color of paper bags his face
a darker crisp as if he was dipped
in mango juice; if we could not find him
he was across the street tinkering like
a mechanic or a chemist with a mélange
of oil and grease he would place beneath
his truck; as children his tool shed was
our playground with enlarged inner tubes
and overgrown truck tires; he bought us
a portable pool so we could slosh and he
could watch us and one day my grandpa
with no name grander than any father
the one with a velvet fedora and cashmere
overcoat was attached to a bed and we
did not see him as much and grandma said
he is resting and I would rub my fingers
through his hair and even though he didn't

want to rest this is what grandpas do they go
off and they rest but he will still have cashews
and quarters in his pocket and when I miss him
I rub my fingers through his hair and ask for a
quarter or I will play dress up in his overcoat
or use his tie pin inherit his taste and his style
he left me that day but I found him in my character
and in this poem

death penalty

he is someone's child
with a mother
a mosquito shudder
raising him in the muck
she labors beneath the sun
like all mothers do
payments due
she is due justice
she is due time
she is due
what about her
what about what
she has to go through
she went through
nine months
punches and kicks
riding on the back
of her hips
backbreaking
she went down
below sand cut

she went to the river
to the lake
quaking these tremors
tree limbs and
femurs
and yes I am crying
and yes I am singing
and yes I am praying
she is due
a river a delivery
she dies for nine months
it was a blunt force
it is hoarse baying
it's a may flower
it's a dowry
out of me
out of me
out of me
it's the sun
it's the sun
it's the sun
under
under
under

the cement block
under the cinder
under the sinner
under the sender
lock me
lock me
it's a Glock
it's a Glock
it's a mock trial
it's a mock trial
it smells foul
it's a mock trial
its smell could
fixin' his plate
fixin' his plate
sealing his fate
sealing his fate
render all
render all
under the cinderblock
under the doomsday clock
with all this soot
from the sugar mill
from all this root
from this everlasting rain

and yes I am crying
and I am singing
and yes I am crying
he is someone
I am someone's child
and her legs are spread
like the Pahokee canal
and she is due
time is due
she is due
she
is due
and he is someone's child
and someone will have to pray
and someone will have to pay
for the blood of the migrants
and no one will lay hands

the testimony against Gertrude Stein

if Schiaparelli and Prada had an impossible conversation
then it was our wait in the Neue Galerie so we trump
back to Demarchelier for avocado and crab on the plate
this memorial day heat of overwhelming crowds
people pushing for place in compartments and gawking
at the multitudinous but I'd rather see Rodin's Eve
as she shuns the camera but continues to be slammed
by arms and big backpacks as all my energy focuses
on maintaining space keeping pace with the merry-
go-round of my own interpretation trying to appreciate
but the docent's eyes depreciate me in value in places
like this I am here with the nude women in the mirror
there is so much to see but there is no clearance if only
I could travel to Paris and take a camera maybe an
introduction to Picasso or Toulouse-Lautrec had my limit-
check with all these vacationers all this impatience
left saying had visited as I sat among the Islamic
pitying myself felt freer with the name Dürer
the man hidden behind the bedsheets as she admires
herself as she conspires with her vanity rather than

acquaint us with Urs Graf and Schongauer
the man with a hat gazing upwards
so I finished the visitation with an Aachen and departed
with Raphael just like Tobias

Letter to my journey

did not write a nine eleven poem
a little after seven stepped on the
ferry witnessing the traffic of the high
sea the indigent the immigrant
the paralytic the decrepit the man
with deformed face the woman
seeking grace

fell into the emotion of the day
the mourning the event taking
place a fat man stood above the
crowd a loud voice commanding
"don't forget, don't forget"

it was as if I was transported back
to the holocaust or the middle
passage Ellis Island had to witness
the shouting the proud the piracy
the booty the conspiracy the woman
with a armful of children
the transparency

did not write a nine eleven poem
but a little after seven she stood
there looking at the statue
the rapture of the waves the
liberty forgotten the rotten injustice
the ferry was airtight the hopeless
the plight

her fall reminded me of
a similar metaphor an internal
implosion the blood the gore
the decadence the extravagance
the manipulated the shallow
the current the past
the last will never follow
the twin lights in the distance
the twisted intolerance the baby
is silent

her fall inconvenienced me
I had my plans my route mapped
out met my friends she stopped
this display it was time
to let self get in the way

the jumping of the train

time will have to stop
before the train leaves Canal Street
and makes it to Union Square
it could be any day now
any moment
the plants are in bloom
out of season the reason
the mountains are bald
and it doesn't matter to you
as long as you think you are
protected from the rats
in Washington Square Park
the condos and the square feet
near Waverly Place
but Lorraine Hansberry burned
crosses there and Richard Wright
made an exodus
but you are on trial
and this train could jump
any second that I am riding
the black bear and the gray wolf

smelling salt the wrought iron
fences suffocating tree blocks
I thought I was dead
instead I came back to right
but I am still to the left
behind all of this pain
behind all this acid fame
and you might just think
this environmental
or economic terrorism
in tow and I am banking on it
at least my family will have millions
at least my children are secure
but no one is safe
not even you

I am scared
from this smoking bus
see the vapors
see the lastingness of
nothingness
shall we pray shall we stay

after the hurricane
after the pines trees
in Vancouver disappear
maybe I will recycle my plastic
relocate and become monastic
it was just a two minute palpitation
and doors murmur
and I left the train
left it in the hands of God
to deliver me once again
because I am in sin
and can't forget

the corner street

the man sitting squatted near the fruit vendor
with his head down listening to the standards and
classics as the sidewalk became bop while
old albums of Pickett and Donna riddle the
summer the bananas are like lost sneakers in
the jazz on the pavement and there is only
wanderlust the bust of smells of Asian
and Thai and I try not to look try not to hear
only want to walk past all the commotion of
ongoing traffic but there is no way to contain
this in a frame shop this is a bursting of another
water main so cars have to park to one side
want to walk slow to feel each moment
before I make it out the store

hostage for eighteen minutes

she said I could not go on the train for another eighteen minutes
my old school ways would never disrespect my elders
would never call anyone out by their name but she behind glass
speaking to me through microphone speaking in drones
her late night gig monotone her nightcap of a watchman
or should I say watch-person had a chance to use her power
a wallflower waiting to tango or wrangle with someone

I politely stood on street level as people made Harlem the collage
as pieces of the street were torn in rips as people on stroll and sail
as people telling the night to stay on for a few more hours but
I could not hang with the late night musicians the ones that play
the standards over at Red Rooster or Paris Blue the ones that
move in circles and burp off cheap hooch in a plastic cup

the night was hot and women on display the shorter the better
the weather had them stripping themselves like paint I could see
clear up her street with the daisy dukes it was so salacious
as I stood there for eighteen more minutes had to finish this
song that haunts me had to diminish the feeling that confronts
me had heard all the musicians talking in the back of the room

how they had a gig at the shrine had a gig downtown only I
was a verbal musician had not signed a contract had only my
body as instrument my throat is Parker's saxophone and lungs
were in the mood of Monk

but in those eighteen minutes the street became classic as I stood
on Lenox rinsing the sweat from the back of my skull had held
my wait in this push and pull the late night of nowhere the thorough-
fare of musicians be it musical or phonetician had held me there
for eighteen more minutes

at the top of the stairs

give a brother some money
for a cup of coffee I'm hungry
Said the man at the top of the stairs
the marble of the Astor Library
the fifth avenue traffic vanities
and the occasional insanity
the crossroad with oxcarts
for books and references
wires and exhibits took
their public space to private
these souls we call vagrants
we try to hide behind our words
of feigned sophistication
as if they do not exist but
what happens when they
make your bathroom a campground
the McGraw Rotunda their pulpit
those first edition and hanging tapestries
can't protect you from them
storming your Bastille
and the blind poet John Milton
sees all and he feel for them

he is the one claiming the reading room
he is the one naming it armageddon
your closed off ropes are merely
a joke because I am grass-rooted
not museum wall highfalutin

the man at the top of the stairs
took me on a tour without docent
without closest advisor where is his
biography where are the alms giving
I understood before the library was
built it was a reservoir so it's natural
for the people to come back to
the water the salmon swimming up-
stream release them from their hatcheries
latch keys of language

the man at the top of the stairs held
me in his grip I knew I would be greeted
at the Carrère stairwell with wine
and brie and the key to a private
lavatory with frames and hand sanitizers
chamomile and lavender

he stood there and waited for me
as I crossed the revolving door
as the emotion in me became strained
I needed to practice what I preached
I needed to seek higher than the facades
he stood there and waited like Lazarus
standing near a gate licking his wounds
his wounds became my wounds his news
became my news I shuffled back to
the depression to prohibition
to brother can you spare a dime
which had the fever of yellow journalism

had to keep some flame alive never knew
where it came from but maybe it was the
man on that elevation as simple as that
his voice his character his choice his manner
he just wanted some crumbs but we will
call him a bomb and at-risk we will
malign him and confine him but he's
always near the door reminding me
as it revolves and I evolve in the calling

Robert Gibbons is an American poet with a lyrical style whose work focuses on issues of social inequality, love, loss and family. He grew up in Belle Glade, Florida, the eldest of five children, and earned a B.S. in History from Florida A&M. In 2007, he moved to New York City in search of his muse, Langston Hughes. Gibbons has studied with such master poets as Cornelius Eady, Marilyn Nelson, Klmiko Hahn and Nathalie Handal, and has participated in workshops at Cave Canem and the 92Y. In addition to teaching English at an East Harlem high school, Gibbons has led youth drama camps and theater programs in Florida, Washington, D.C., and New York City. His work has been published in numerous anthologies, including *Hellstrung and Crooked* (Uphook Press), *The Brownstone Poets Anthology*, *Dinner with the Muse* (Ra Rays Press), *The Cartier Street Review*, *Nomad's Choir*, and *Maintenant 6: A Journal of Contemporary Dada Art & Literature* (Three Rooms Press). His poetry may also be heard on the CD *Brain Ampin'* (Logo Chrysalis Productions).

books on three rooms press

POETRY

by Hala Alyan
Atrium

by Peter Carlaftes
DrunkYard Dog
I Fold with the Hand I Was Dealt

by Joie Cook
When Night Salutes the Dawn

by Thomas Fucaloro
Inheriting Craziness is Like
  a Soft Halo of Light

Patrizia Gattaceca
Soul Island

by Kat Georges
Our Lady of the Hunger
Punk Rock Journal

by Robert Gibbons
Close to the Tree

by Karen Hildebrand
One Foot Out the Door
Take a Shot at Love

by Matthew Hupert
Ism is a Retrovirus

by Dominique Lowell
Sit Yr Ass Down or You Ain't gettin
  no Burger King

by Jane Ormerod
Recreational Vehicles on Fire
Welcome to the Museum of Cattle

by Susan Scutti
We Are Related

by Jackie Sheeler
to[o] long

by The Bass Player from Hand Job
Splitting Hairs

by Angelo Verga
Praise for What Remains

by George Wallace
Poppin' Johnny
EOS: Abductor of Men

PHOTOGRAPHY-MEMOIR

by Mike Watt
On & Off Bass

FICTION

by Michael T. Fournier
Hidden Wheel

DADA

Maintenant: Journal of
Contemporary Dada Art & Literature
(Annual poetry/art journal, since 2003)

SHORT STORIES

Have a NYC: New York Short Stories
Annual Short Fiction Anthology

HUMOR

by Peter Carlaftes
A Year on Facebook

PLAYS

by Madeline Artenberg &
Karen Hildebrand
The Old In-and-Out

by Peter Carlaftes
Triumph For Rent (3 Plays)
Teatrophy (3 More Plays)

by Larry Myers
Mary Anderson's Encore
Twitter Theater

TRANSLATIONS

by Patrizia Gattaceca
Isula d'Anima / Soul Island
(poems in Corsican with
English translations)

by George Wallace
EOS: Abductor of Men (American
poems with Greek translations)

three rooms press | new york, ny
current catalog: www.threeroomspress.com

CPSIA information can be obtained
at www.ICGtesting.com
Printed in the USA
FFOW04n1250200115
10374FF

9 780988 400818